How Great Leaders Build Great Teams!

Simple, Actionable Tips

By: Jennifer Takagi

Table of Contents:

Foreword

As a workplace leader and builder of teams, have you ever asked yourself, "Why is it so hard to engage my employees? What will it take to promote increased performance and productivity? How can I more effectively connect with my team?"

If so, then your questions and concerns are about to be addressed and answered.

A long-time fan of Jennifer Takagi's training style, I've already benefitted from the expertise she shares with her readers.

Enjoy reading this book, implementing Jennifer's guidelines, and creating your own leadership legacy.

Donna Rynda
Owner- Trainer- Speaker
Make It Matter, Inc.

Chapter 1:
Why Isn't It Just About The Work?

For many years, I was responsible for collecting all the data in preparation for the quarterly goals report. None of the computer programs were set up to generate a report that corresponded to the goals, although, the goals were national and every office's benchmarks were the same. It should have been a simple process. A button should have been pushed, a report generated and distributed across the nation. However, this is not how it worked.

The task was a little frustrating. I spent a lot of time compiling data and populating the report. I found myself scheduling vacations around goal reporting. Heaven forbid I was ever sick around these four reporting cycles.

Once I completed my portion, I turned it into a colleague in another division. He was responsible for compiling the data from all the divisions and submitting the finalized report. It was all about the work with him, and we struggled to communicate. I had little appreciation for what he was tasked to do. He had little understanding of the work being performed in my division or how I had to compile the data. We both dreaded having to interact.

My nemesis and I worked on opposite ends of the building. However, we were on a team because we each contributed to a combined report. I felt I had ownership because I provided valuable information for it. He felt as if he had ownership because he compiled all the data into one cohesive document and sent it forward. We were both right.

Luckily for both of us our office held a training session on different behavioral styles. We took a simple assessment and looked at the four basic styles. Once we explored each style, we considered how conflicts could arise if you were dealing with someone different from yourself.

The majority of frustrations at work come from the interactions with others rather than the work itself. If we understand how we operate, our similarities as well as our differences, we can have more productive exchanges and not dread them.

Chapter 2:

Is There A Fix For My Employees?

Understanding behavior is essential to creating a cohesive team. As a leader, you must understand your team members. How do they communicate? What gifts and talents do they bring to the table? Are there "gaps" in their abilities? If gaps are present, how do you want to address them? Is it possible to have someone else complete certain tasks? Is training needed to bring those skills up to par?

Maybe those gaps are your fault. Maybe they have never been shown how to complete the task. It might be they are doing the best they can because the workload distribution is not even. It's possible they've not been able to spend enough time on the specific project to produce the expected outcome.

What if you didn't provide specific guidance and step-by-step instructions? As an employee, it was a horrible feeling to work hard on a project to have it rejected by your boss because it wasn't what he/she wanted. You thought you were doing exactly what was asked, but alas, the instructions were not clear.

I remember my boss being cross with me because the outcome of a project was not what she had envisioned. When she chastised me for failing to ask for assistance when I didn't understand her instructions, I was dumbfounded. I had followed the instructions to the letter. Unfortunately, she hadn't fully formulated her vision before she gave those instructions. Being the leader means you have to provide directions so your vision is realized.

Knowing your team will assist you with the task of providing those instructions. If you understand how each team member responds to guidance, you have a greater chance of receiving what you really want. Someone who is detail-oriented will not perform well when given very high-level instructions that are really more of an overview of what you "sort of" expect. Likewise, employees who can almost read your mind will not appreciate detailed instructions. Communicating so you understand and are understood will build that cohesive team. Employees meet or exceed your expectations when you speak the same language.

Chapter 3:
Learn To Be Great!

We all know the egotistical boss. The one who shouts orders and demands everyone know exactly what is expected just because the order was given. Much to their surprise, projects are not completed on time. The end result is not what was wanted, needed or expected.

Why is this? Lack of communication.

Communication is critical! Great leaders put their egos aside and put their employees first. They are engaging and approachable. The office door is open. Employees feel free to ask questions and clarify instructions. Great leaders want the employees to succeed. Successful employees lead to successful organizations.

People have choices. They know there are great bosses who create cohesive, pleasant environments where they can thrive. Job satisfaction is important. Employees leave good jobs for less pay because they are not appreciated. History shows when employees are treated with respect and appreciated, everyone performs at a higher level.

I overheard a conversation where one woman told another she had been told if she bolstered her employees with compliments for doing a good job, they would perform better, but she wasn't going to do it. They were paid to do a job and she should not have to coddle them, nor would she. She demonstrated her ego mattered more than having a satisfied staff. Often, the simplest things to do to be a great leader are overlooked or ignored.

Mark Twain said, *"I can live for two months on one good compliment!"*

Excellent employees know what they appreciate from their boss. As you think back on your career, what leadership qualities made you sit up and take notice? What made you decide you wanted a leadership role in the first place?

You want to succeed. You want to lead the winning team. You want the goals to be met. You want a happy team. One that is more than willing to go the extra mile for you and the organization. You have a decision to make.

Are you going to step up to the plate, or follow the status quo?

What does following the status quo look like?

- Refusing to recognize everyone is a little different, like a snowflake.
- Believing everyone responds to you simply because you are the boss.
- Giving minimal instructions and expecting spectacular results.
- Expecting everyone to react like you do.
- Demanding consistency when you are inconsistent.

What are probable outcomes?

- Frustrated employees who don't understand expectations.
- Discontent employees because they don't respect you or your dictatorial style.
- Missed deadlines.
- Personality conflicts.

- Inconsistent employees and work products.

I ask again: Are you going to step up to the plate, or follow the status quo?

Chapter 4:
Now, Do It!

You want to be the best leader you can be. Most of us do. Are you going to do what it takes to be the best? You can. It takes commitment and access to more information than you have had up until now.

Commit to spending more time with your staff. It is impossible to understand them and their working styles if you spend your entire day in your office with the door closed. I worked with a manager once who discovered she did not have the opportunity to speak to one half of her staff each day because of which door she used. Her simple commitment was to mix up which door she used so throughout the day she had the opportunity to engage with each and every staff member.

Take a few minutes to consider your day. List three things you can begin doing right now to spend more time with your staff.

1. _____

2. _____

3. _____

It is amazing how much more communication happens between two people when you take time to have a conversation. What if your working environment is virtual? It is important to schedule time to talk three times a week with no agenda. You can keep it to 10 minutes or less, but you need to interact.

The next thing you should do is consider their behavioral style. Ask yourself a few questions about each of your team members.

1. Is he/she outgoing or reserved?

2. Does he/she focus more on the relationship or the task at hand?

As a matter of fact, you could/should ask those same questions of yourself.

What do the responses reveal about your employee/yourself?

Outgoing person interacting with a more reserved person:

Let me just say, you/we, can wear them out. Outgoing people are often fast-paced; always on the move. Reserved people consider the situation before responding so they are often slower paced.

Reserved leader with an outgoing person:

Reserved people can consider an outgoing employee as impulsive and quick, too quick to make decisions. The outgoing employee can view the reserved leader as overly cautious. Understanding those simple yet complex differences can make a world of difference in your interactions.

Relationship-focused manager with task-focused employee:

The relationship-focused manager can seem to talk way too much when discussing a project. At least that is how it appears to the task-focused employee. The employee would like you to state the case and move on. They don't necessarily want to connect on a deeper level, but would prefer to go on with the task at hand.

Task-focused manager with relationship-focused employee.

The task-focused manager wants to explain what needs to be done, straight to the point, and move on to the next item on the agenda. The employee can be offended because there was no prelude, no lead-in, and no relationship building before addressing the task at hand.

What if you have an outgoing, relationship-oriented leader and an outgoing, relationship-oriented employee? At first you might think that could be the dynamic made for success. What if they are so busy building the relationship the task is never completed?

Likewise, if you have a reserved, task-oriented manager and a reserved, task-oriented employee, they could never interact and be working on different problems!

Do you see where avoidable conflict can arise? If a mediocre leader takes the short amount of time to understand themselves and their employees, and makes the conscious decision to adapt to those differences, the mediocre can become great.

About the Author:
Meet Jennifer Takagi

Those Were Simple Steps. What Else?

What else can you do to develop your communication and leadership skills to rise to greatness faster?

I am Jennifer Takagi, an Executive Leadership & Communication Coach who teaches leaders how to play well at work so they can drive better performance from people they lead, increase profitability and create a purposeful workplace where people want to come and play—productively.

For 30 years, I've traveled to conference rooms across the country training and teaching. I've covered a lot of miles, but more, I've talked to a lot of people. Many were frustrated people. While their organizational cultures and landscapes differed, the challenges they all faced were similar. Managers felt stagnant and ineffective. Employees felt disconnected,

19

devalued and overworked.   There was no sharing. There was no working together to achieve measurable results. Performance and productivity suffered. On the surface, there was a breakdown in skills.

There was a breakdown between people.

This is where I come in.

My work ties the intrinsic motivators and emotional-social intelligence —the inner stuff—to behavior, employee engagement and performance. Through in-depth assessments and coaching, I help management professionals to understand how their personality types and personal strengths play a role in their leadership style, and how to translate that data into a toolkit that brings the best out of themselves and their employees.

I'll teach you how to put people first.

I'll teach you how to lead from the inside out.
I'll teach you how to become the inspirational, influential and impactful leader you were destined to be.

I'll teach you how to create a workplace where your employees work with you and not just for you.

Because Mom was right.

Playing well together is so much better.

Contact me so we can start your plan to Greatness!

Jennifer Takagi
Jennifer@jtokc.com
www.jennifertakagi.com
405-414-0901

NOTES:

www.ingramcontent.com/pod-product-compliance
Lightning Source LLC
Chambersburg PA
CBHW070303190526
45169CB00004B/1513